BEAUTY in the BIBLE

AN ADULT COLORING BOOK | VOL 2

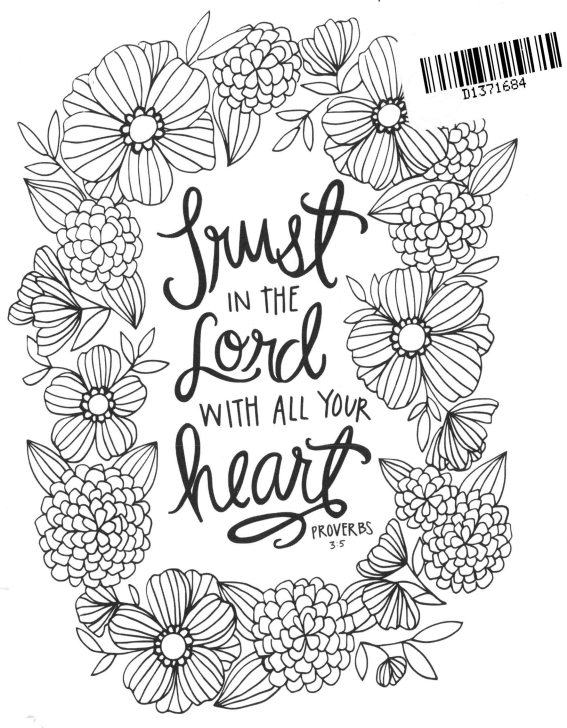

Trust
IN THE
Lord
WITH ALL YOUR
heart

PROVERBS
3:5

PEN + PAINT

paige tate
& CO.

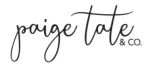

Published in 2016 by Blue Star Press
Paige Tate & Co. is an Imprint of Blue Star Press
PO Box 8835, Bend, OR 97708
contact@paigetate.com
www.paigetate.com

Scripture quotations are from the following:

Scriptures taken from the Holy Bible, New International Version®, NIV®. Copyright © 1973, 1978, 1984, 2011 by Biblica, Inc.™ Used by permission of Zondervan. All rights reserved worldwide. www.zondervan.com The "NIV" and "New International Version" are trademarks registered in the United States Patent and Trademark Office by Biblica, Inc.™

Scripture taken from the New King James Version®. Copyright © 1982 by Thomas Nelson. Used by permission. All rights reserved.

Scripture quotations are from the ESV® Bible (The Holy Bible, English Standard Version®), copyright © 2001 by Crossway, a publishing ministry of Good News Publishers. Used by permission.

ISBN: 9781944515157

Printed in Mexico

17 16 15 14 13 12

hello! WELCOME TO RELAXATION.

We are so excited to get creative with you!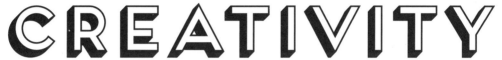

WE ARE PASSIONATE ABOUT INSPIRING

CREATIVITY

IN EVERYONE. WE SIMPLY PROVIDE THE
BEAUTIFUL CANVAS TO IGNITE THE

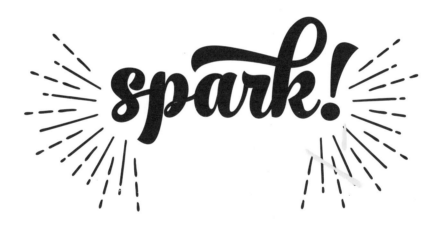

COLOR. FRAME. GIVE.

We've created this book with thick paper and perforated edges so that you color these inspirational prints and easily tear them out, frame them, or give them to a friend! The larger prints fit perfectly in an 8 x 10 frame and the smaller prints are the perfect 5 x 7 to frame or mail!

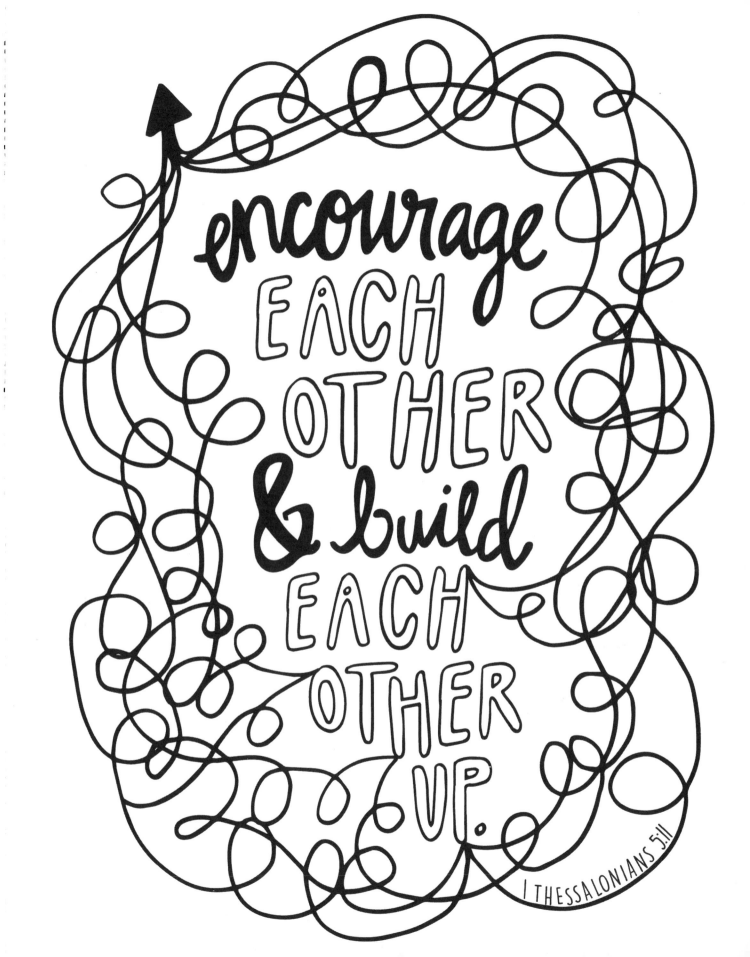

encourage
EACH
OTHER
& build
EACH
OTHER
UP.

1 THESSALONIANS 5:11

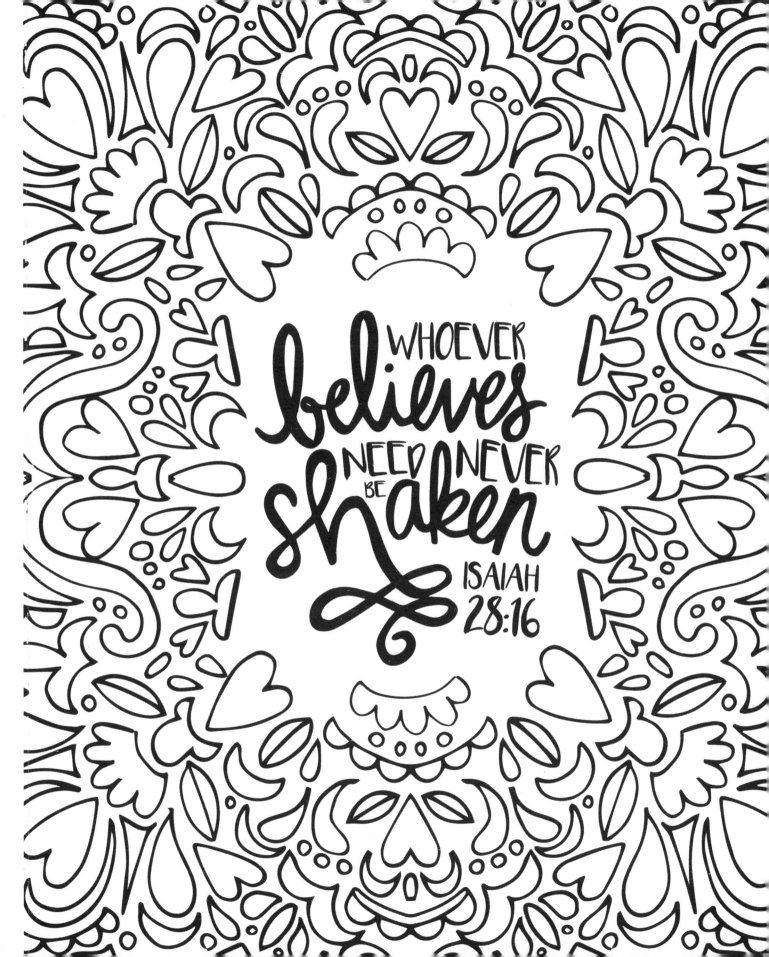

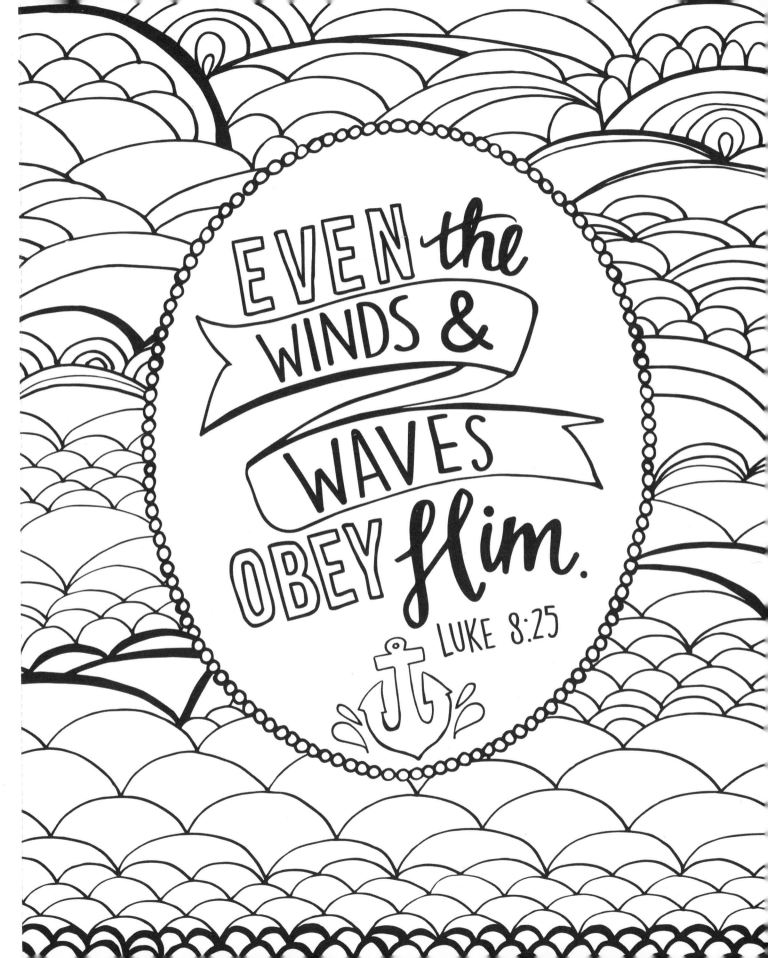

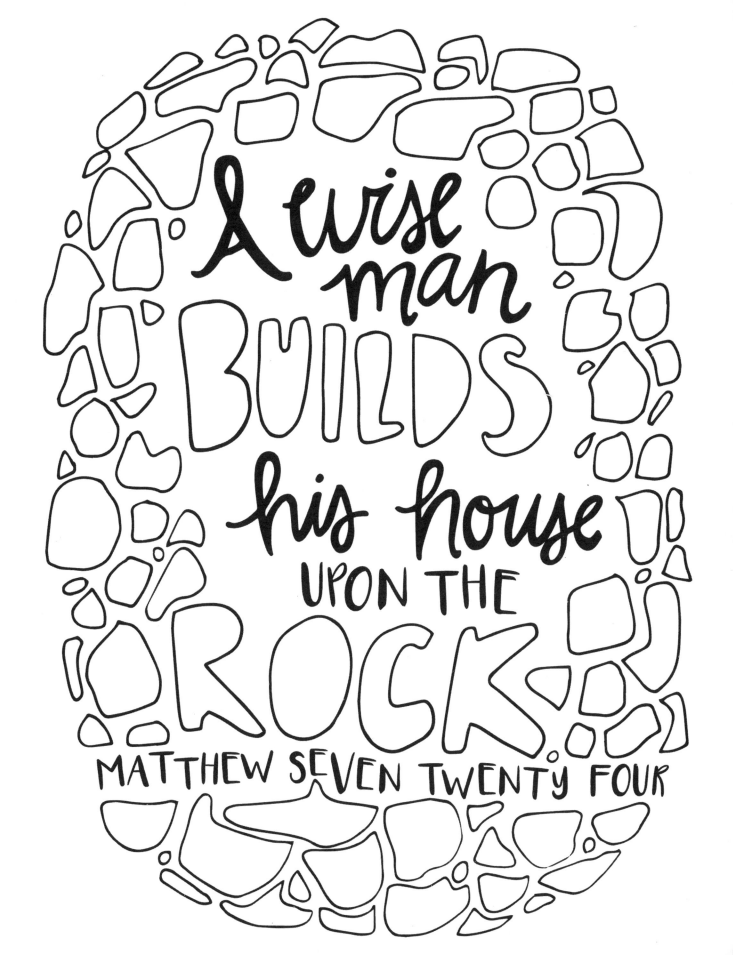

UNLESS THE LORD BUILDS A HOUSE THE WORK OF THE BUILDERS IS WASTED. PSALM 127:1

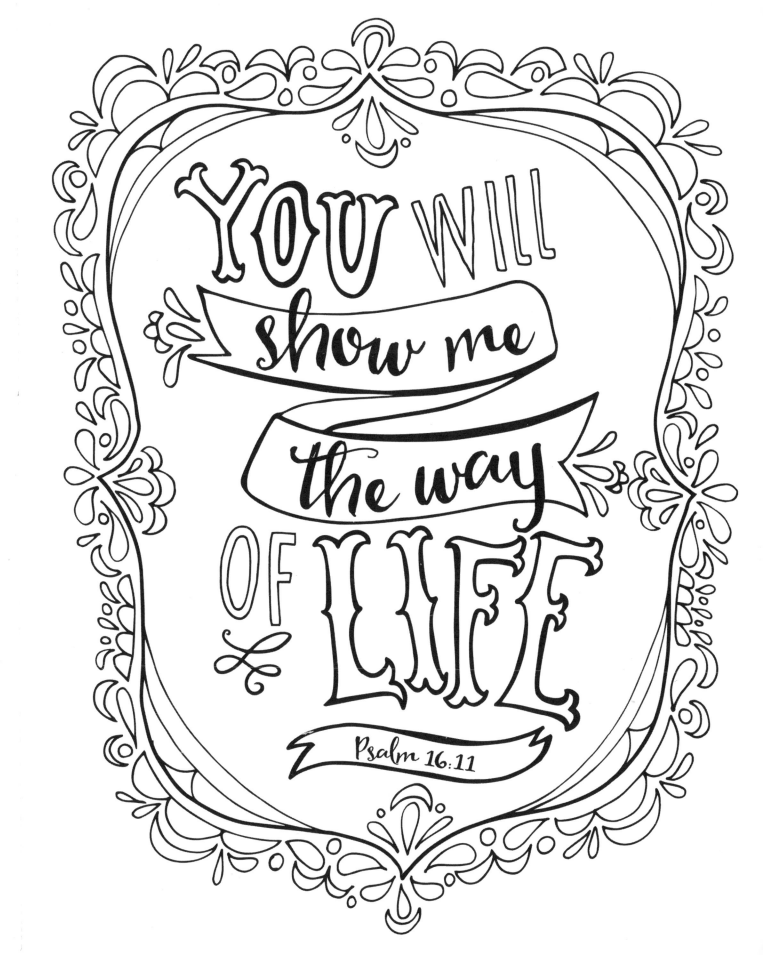

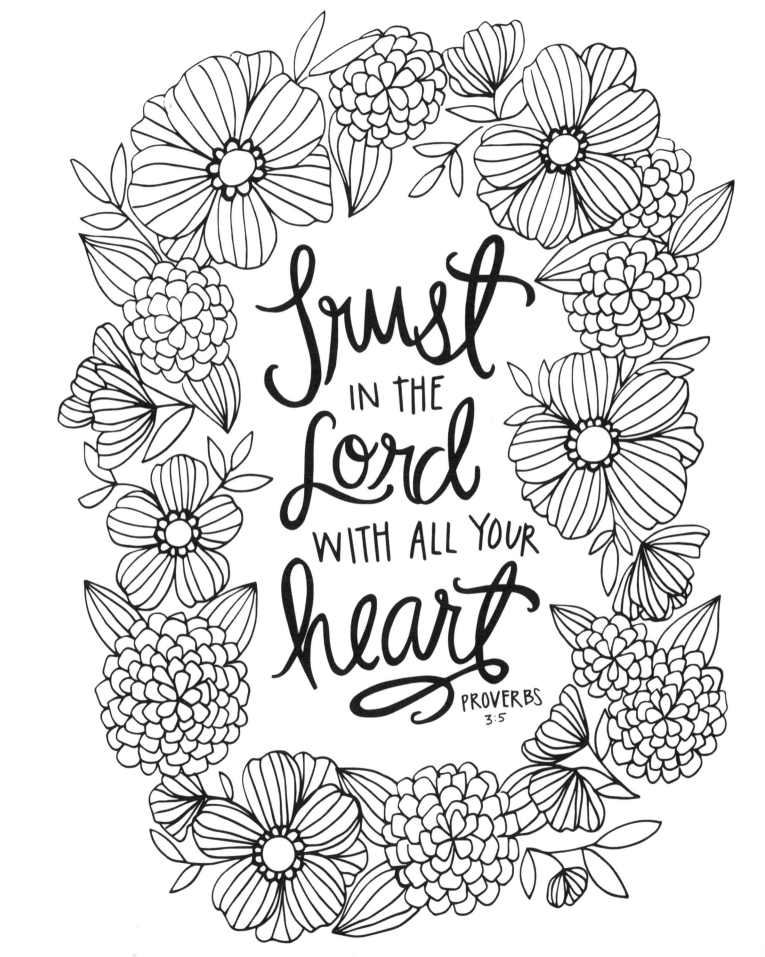

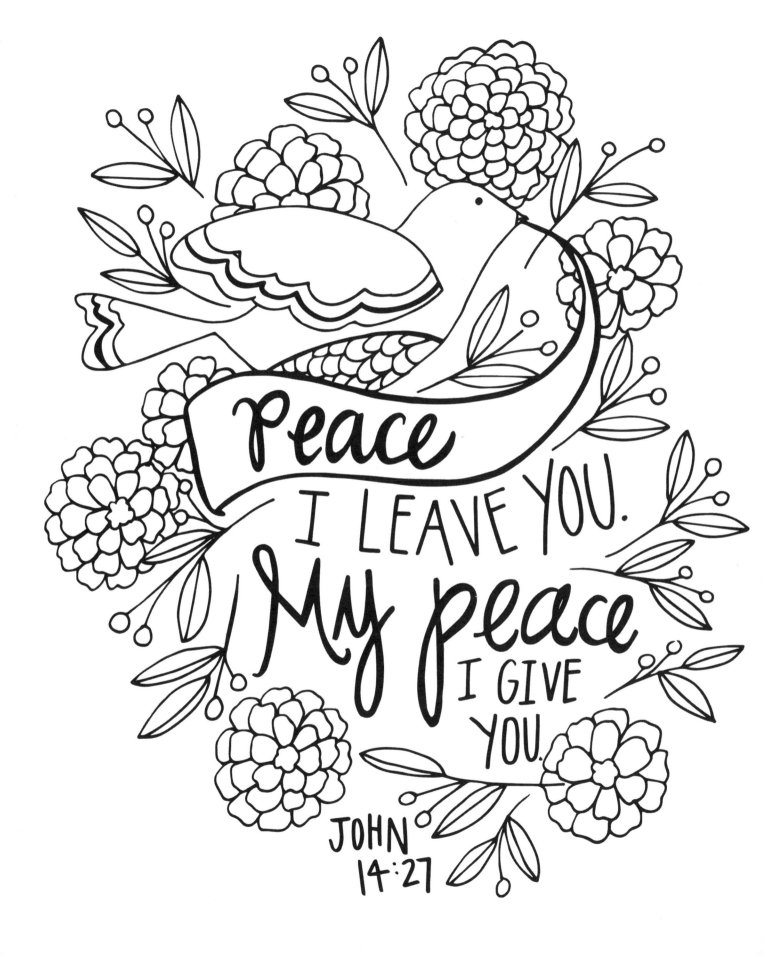

Peace I LEAVE YOU. My peace I GIVE YOU.

JOHN 14:27

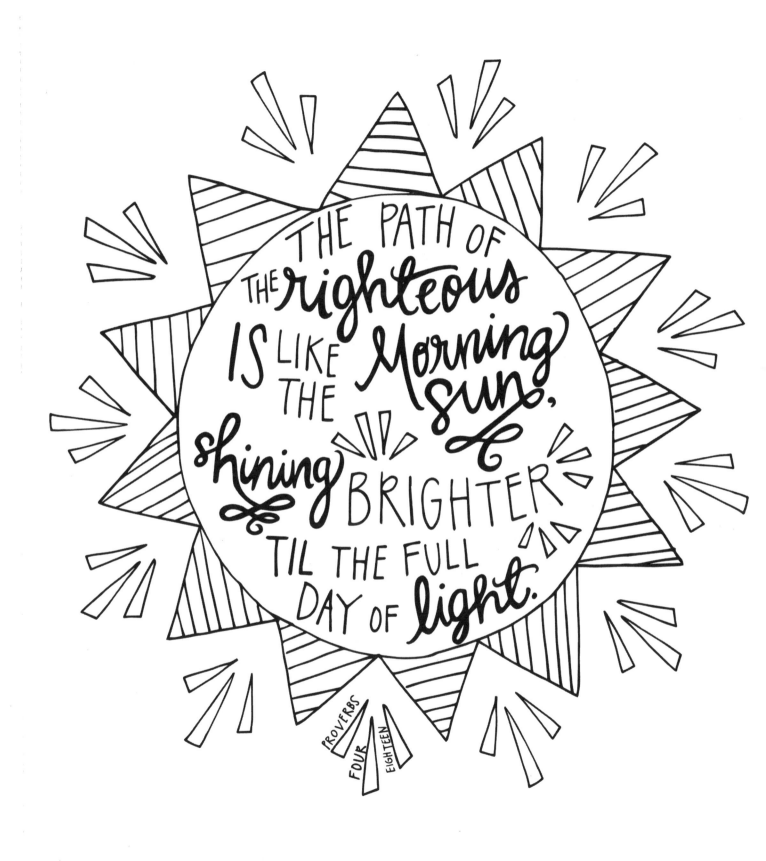

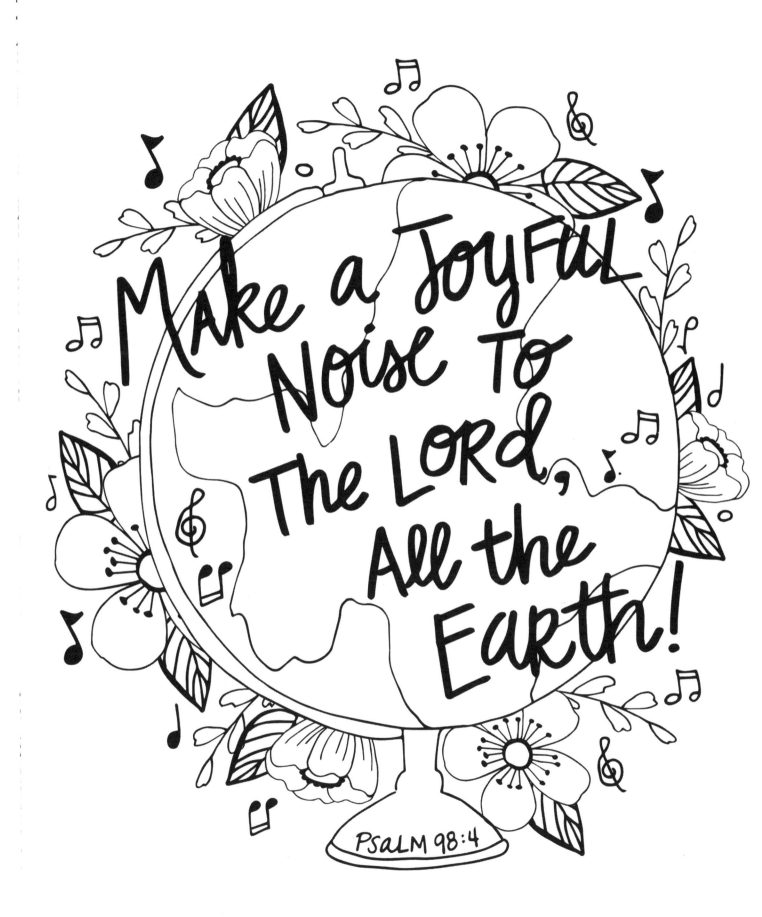

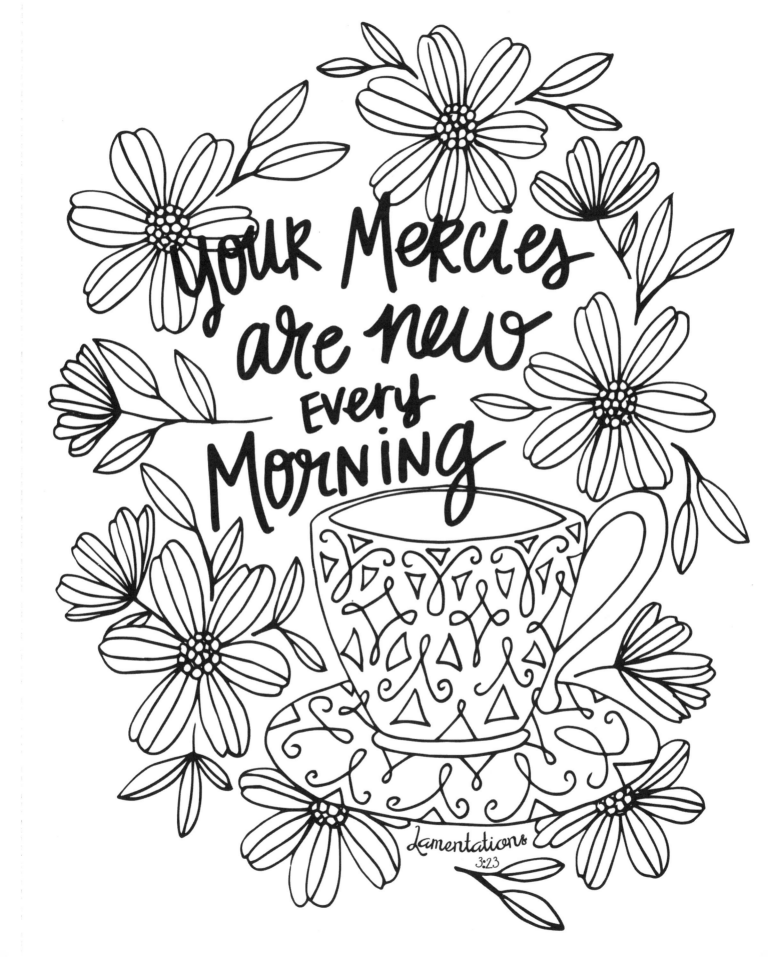

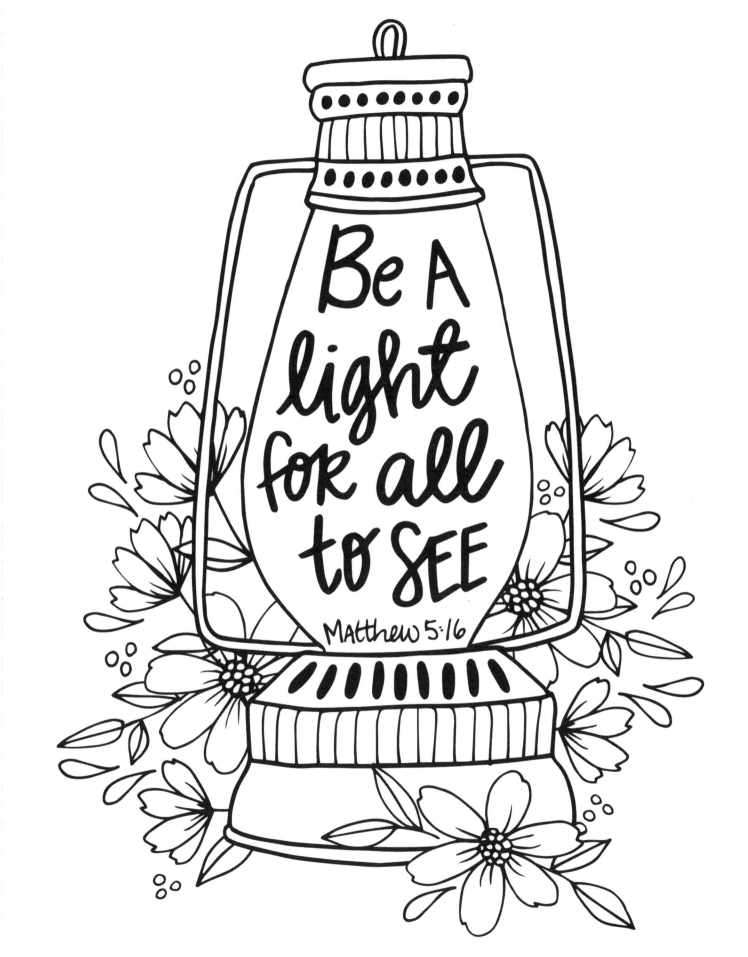

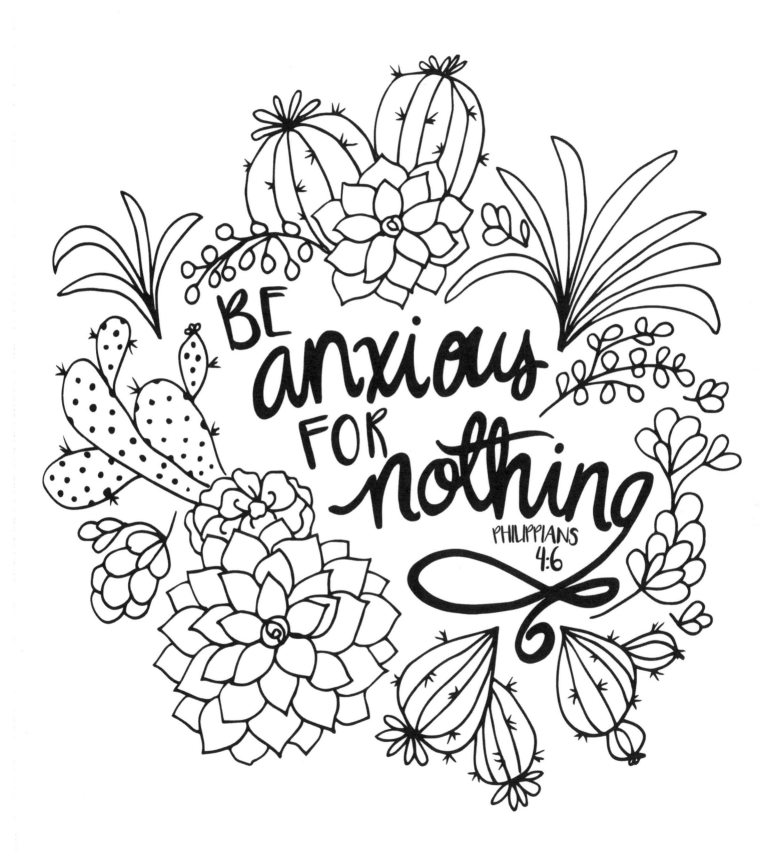

BE anxious FOR nothing

PHILIPPIANS 4:6

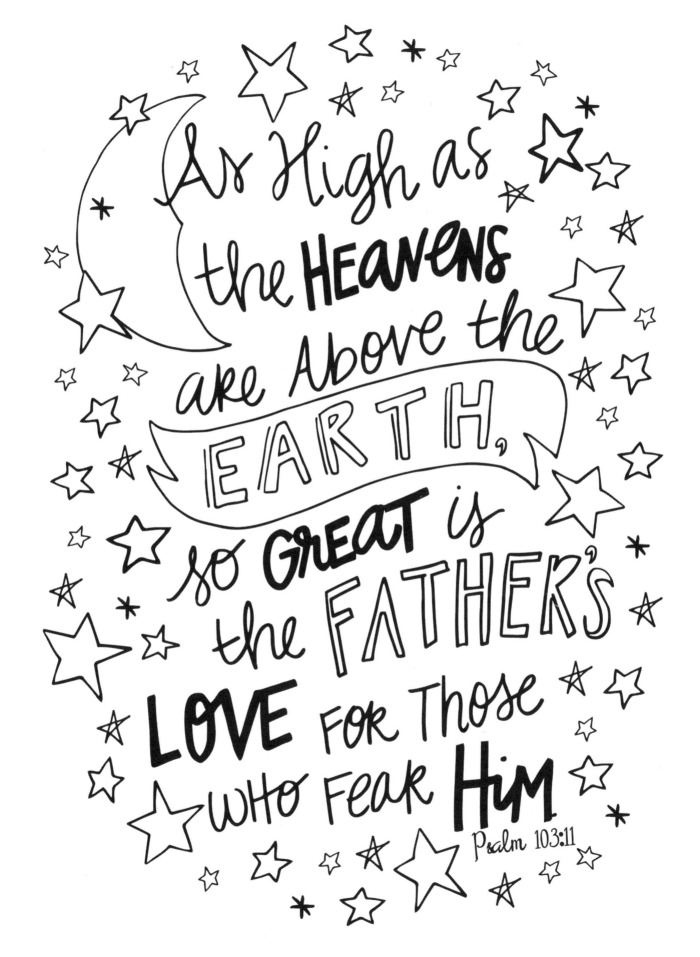

As High as the HEAVENS are Above the EARTH, so GREAT is the FATHER'S LOVE for those who Fear HiM

Psalm 103:11

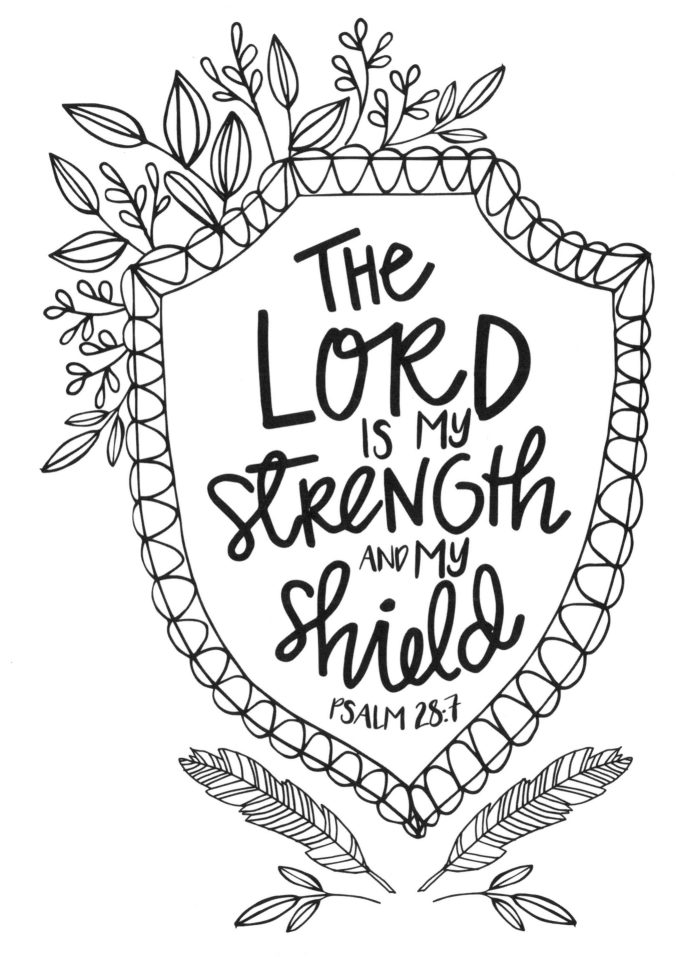

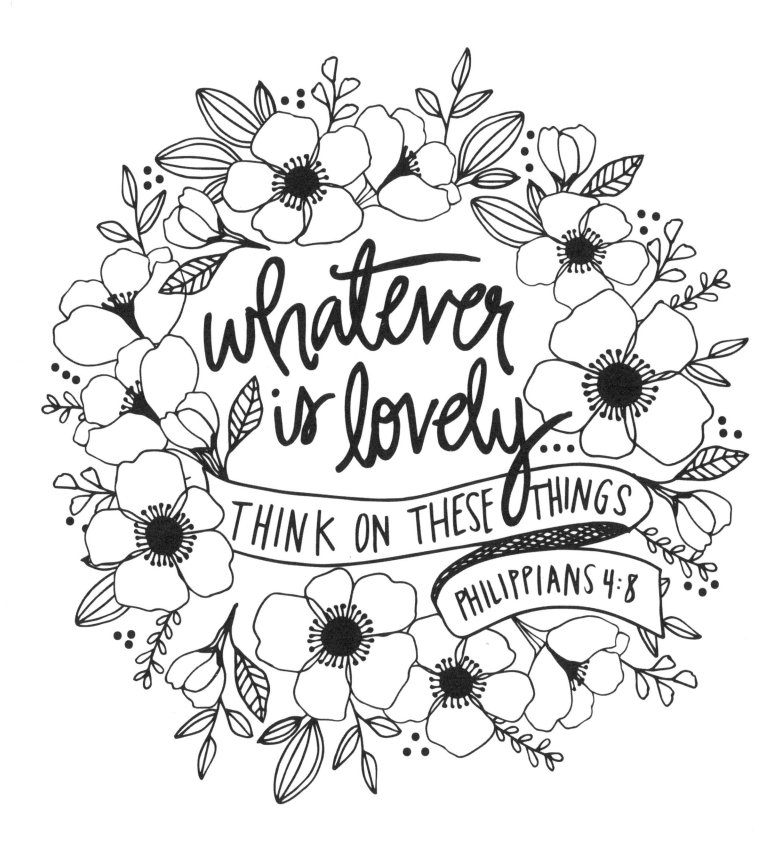

encourage

EACH OTHER

DAILY

WHILE IT IS

still TODAY

HEBREWS 3:13

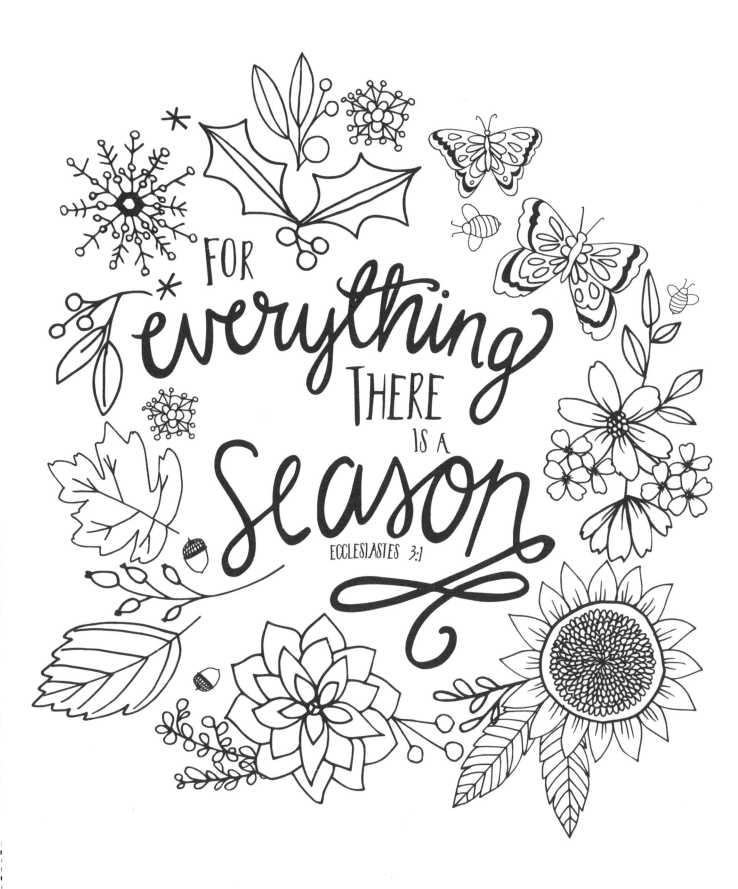

FOR everything THERE IS A season

ECCLESIASTES 3:1

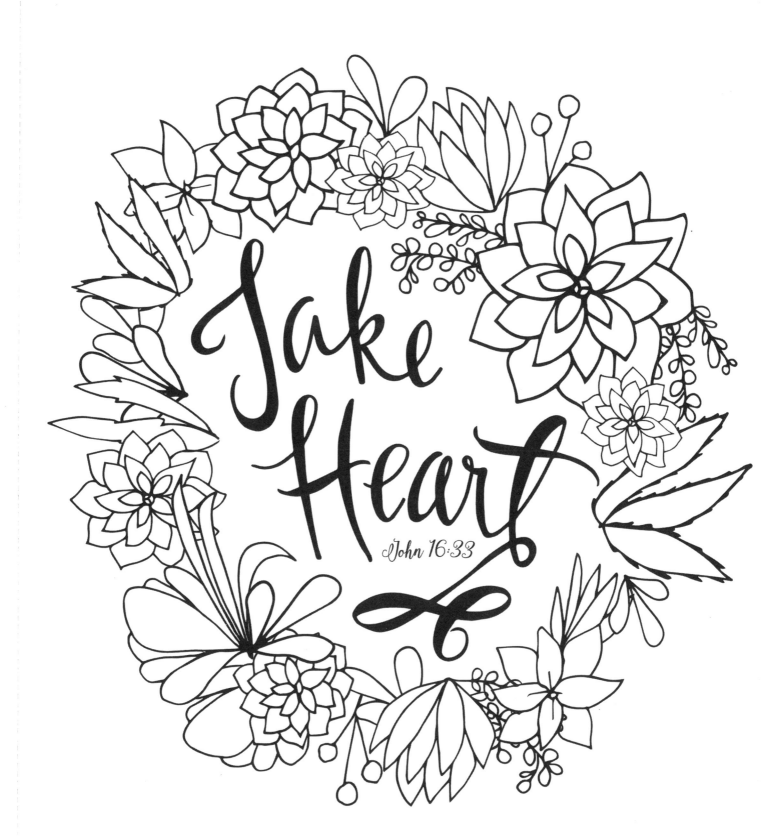

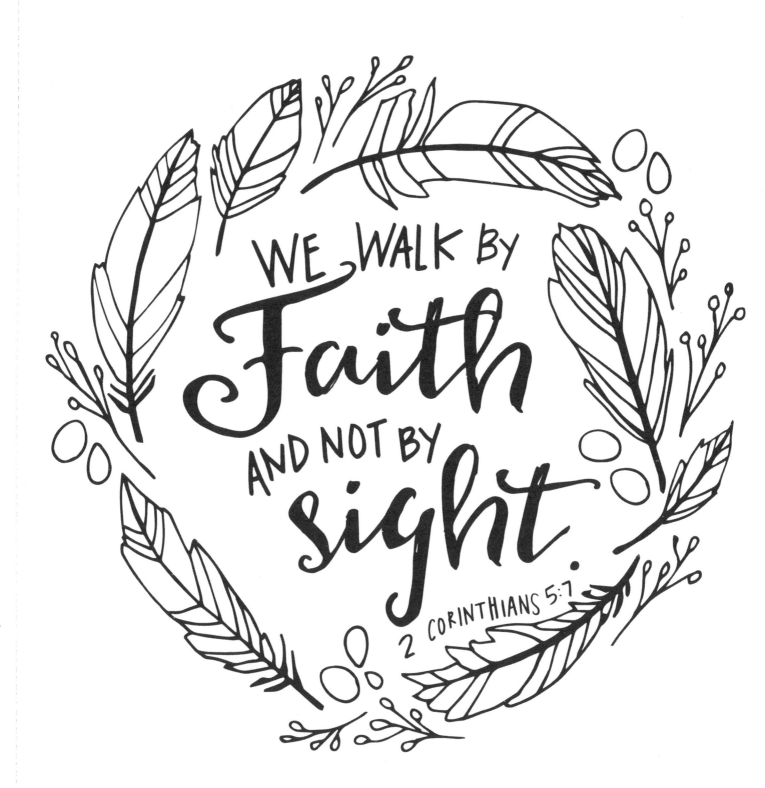

WE WALK BY Faith AND NOT BY sight.

2 CORINTHIANS 5:7

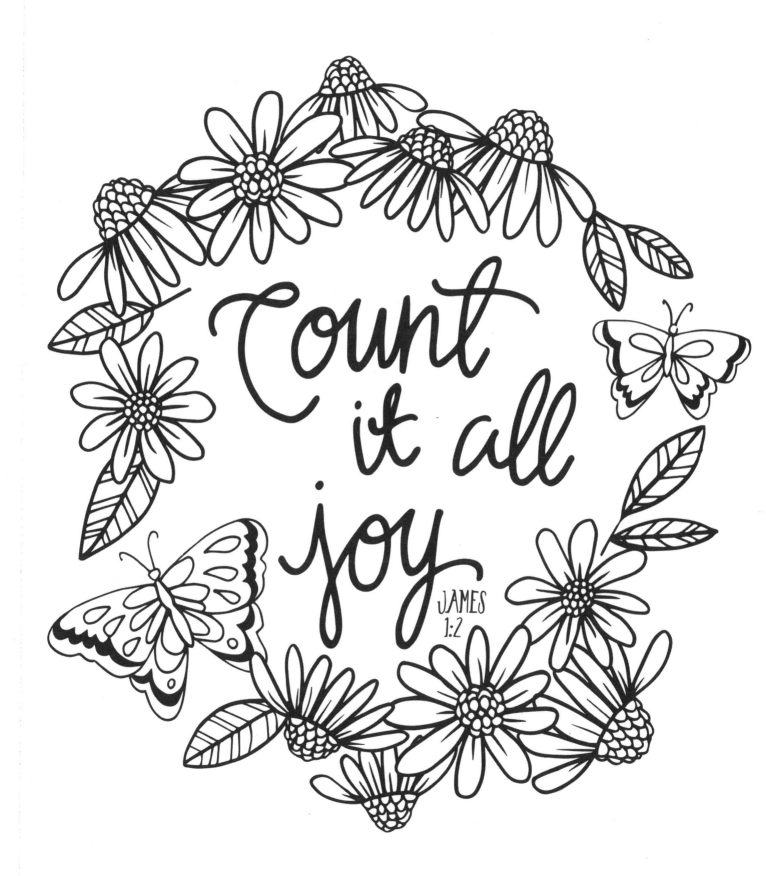

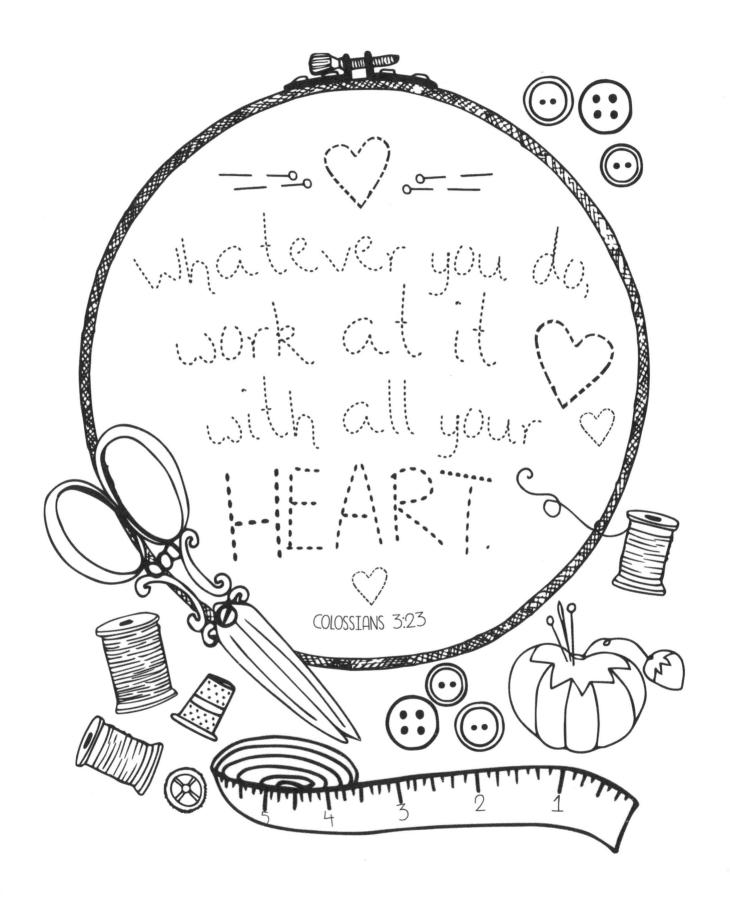

Whatever you do, work at it with all your HEART.

COLOSSIANS 3:23

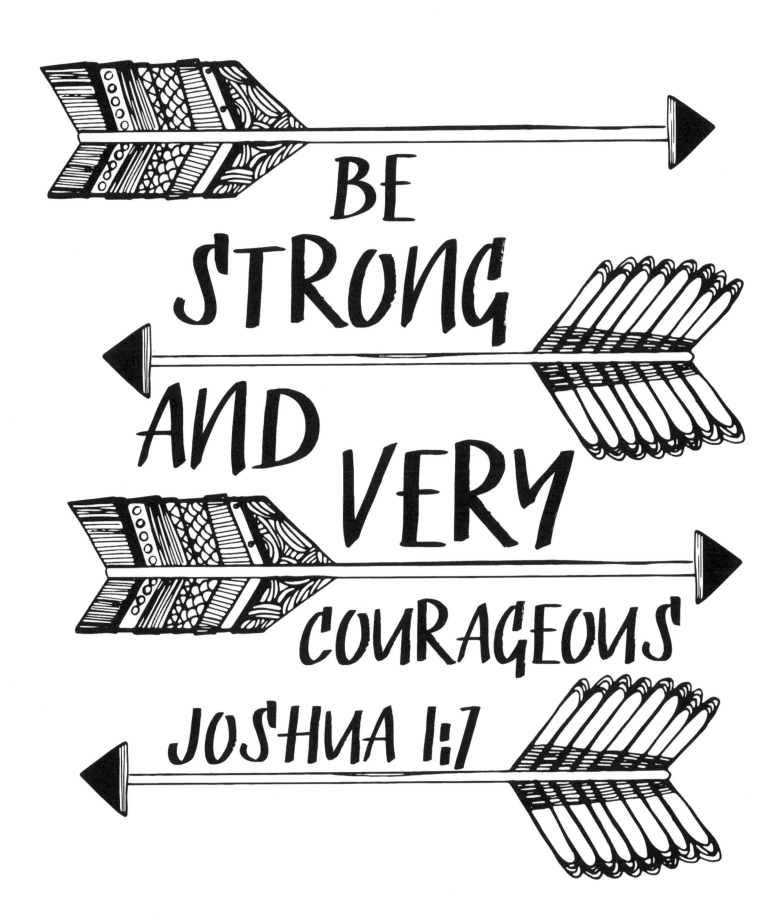

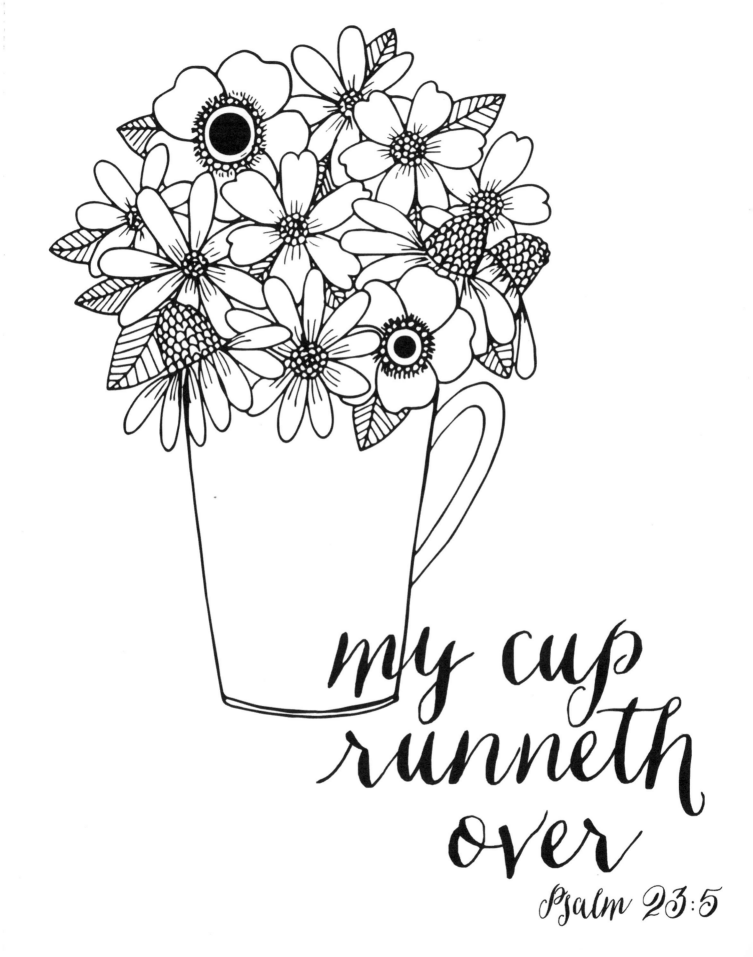

my cup
runneth
over
Psalm 23:5

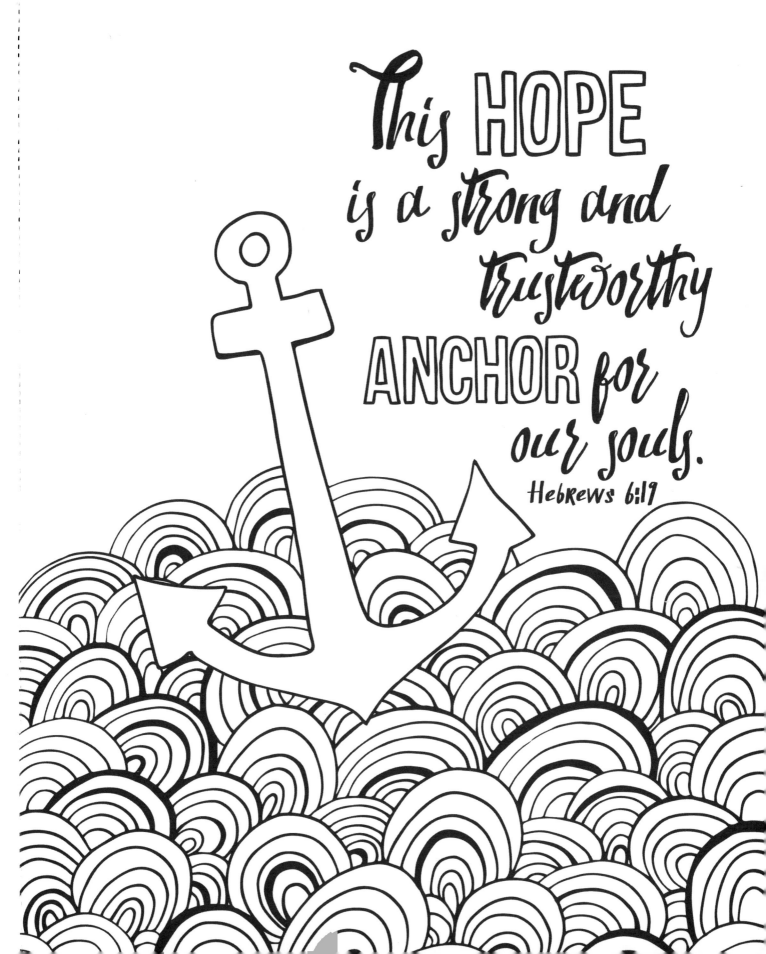

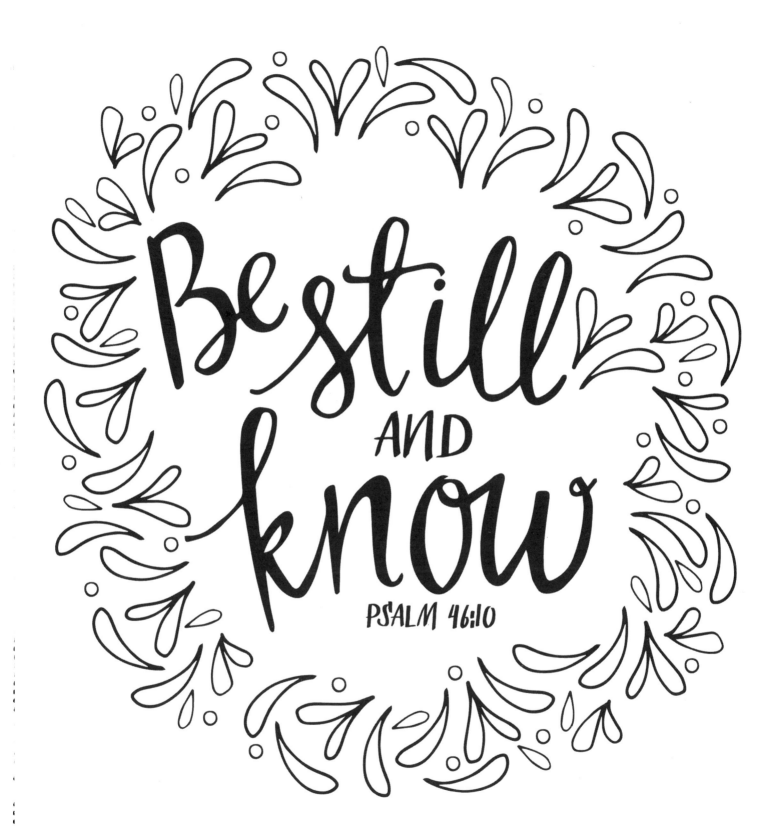

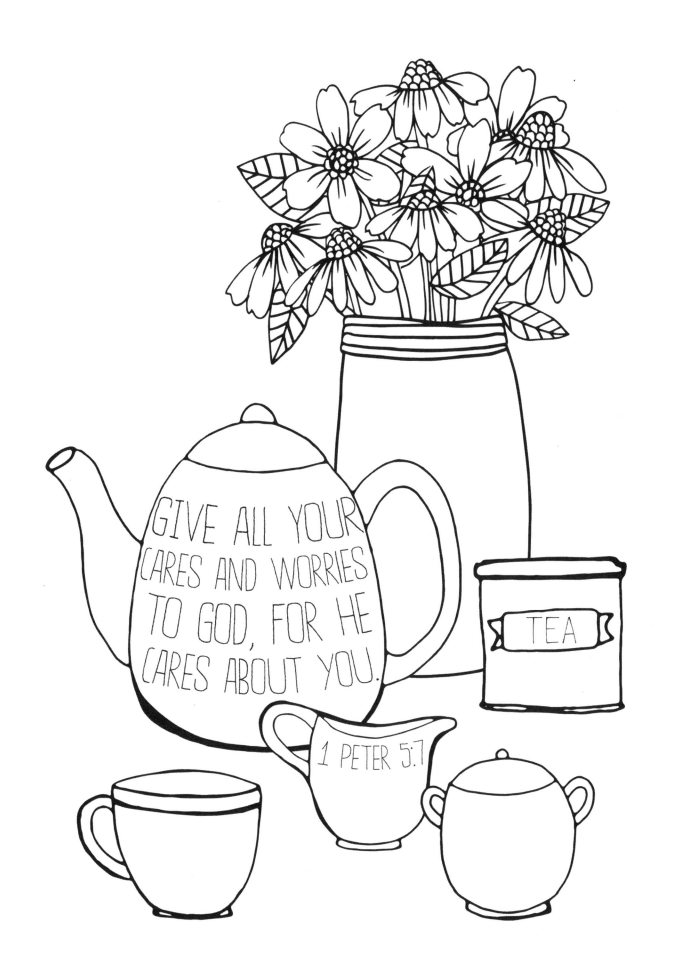

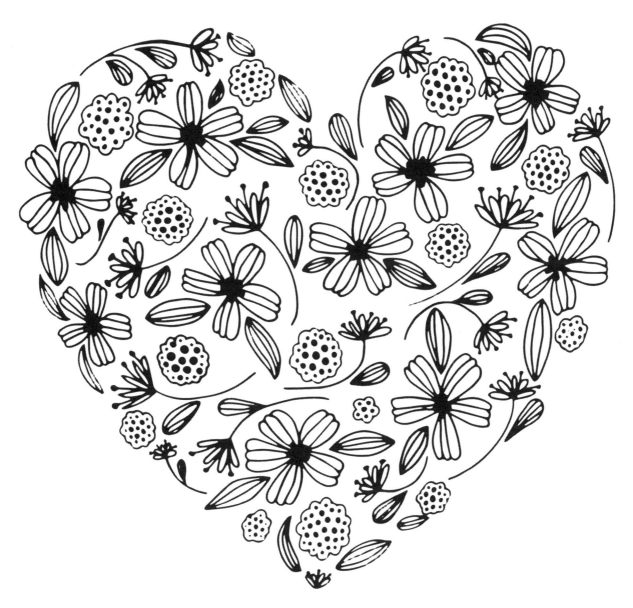

above all else,
guard your heart,
for it is the
wellspring of life.
proverbs 4:23

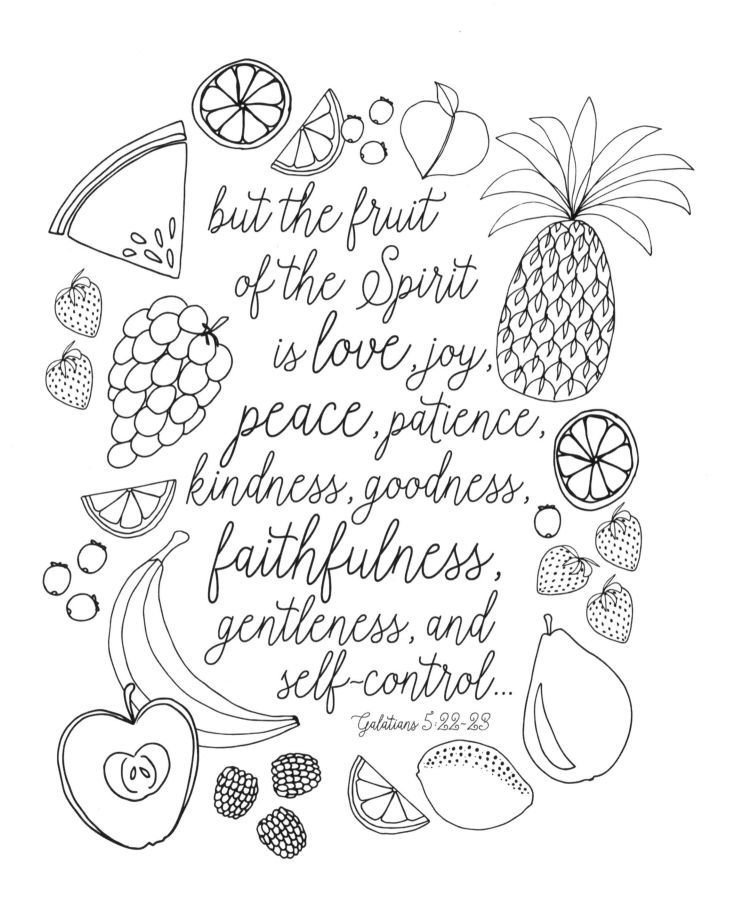

but the fruit of the Spirit is love, joy, peace, patience, kindness, goodness, faithfulness, gentleness, and self-control...

Galatians 5:22-23

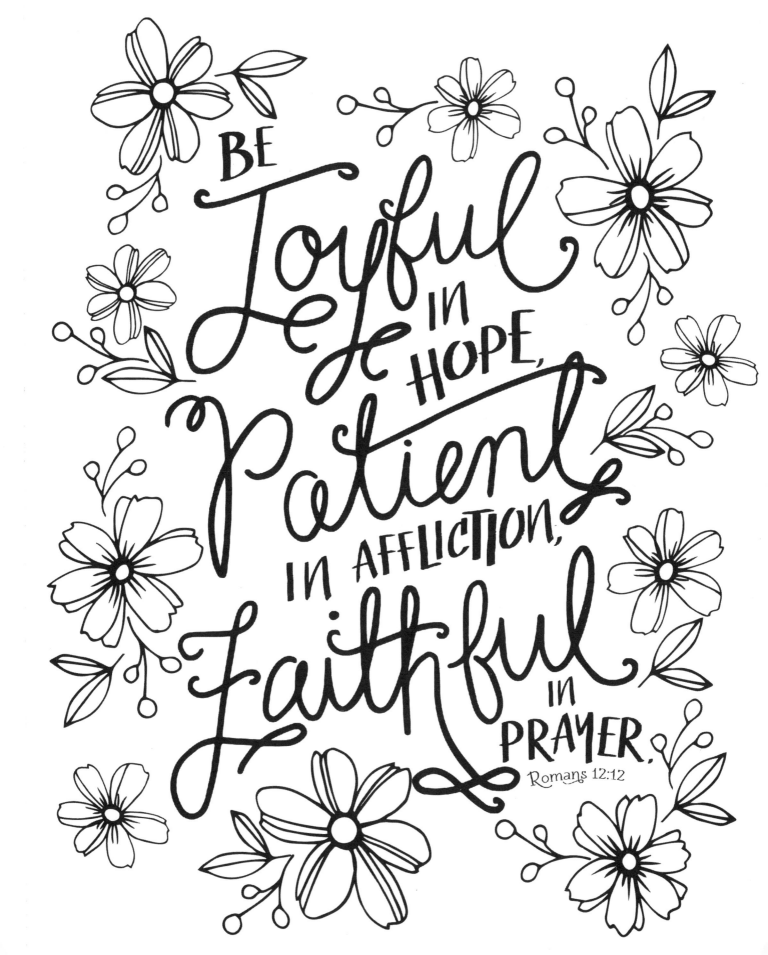

BE Joyful IN HOPE, Patient IN AFFLICTION, Faithful IN PRAYER.

Romans 12:12

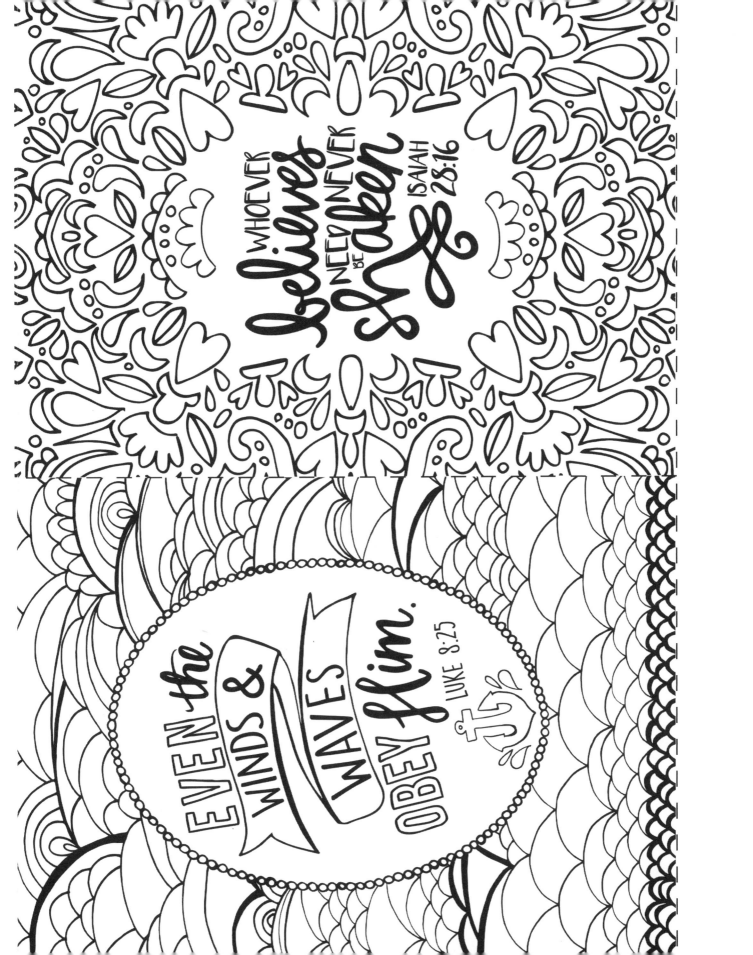

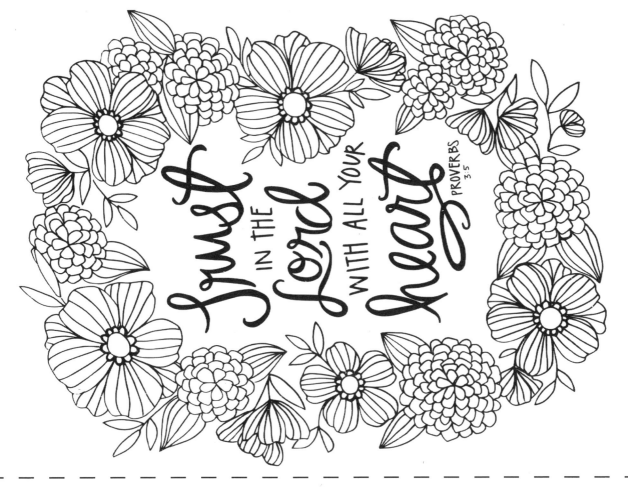

Trust in the Lord with all your heart. PROVERBS 3:5

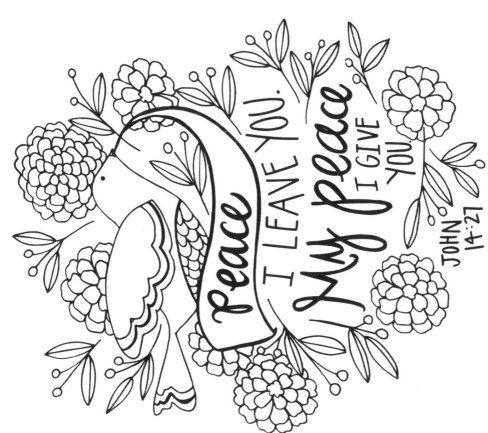

Peace I leave you. My Peace I give you. JOHN 14:27

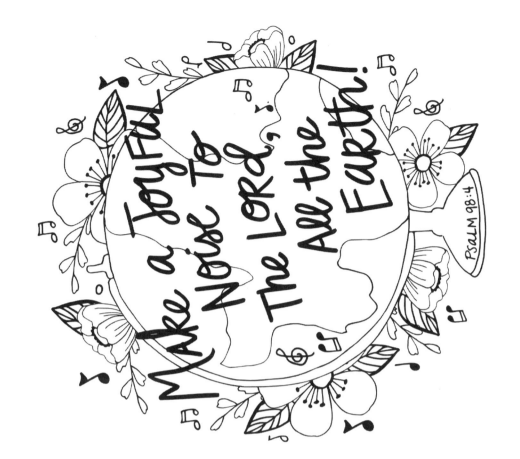

Make a Joyful Noise To The LORD, All the Earth!

Psalm 98:4

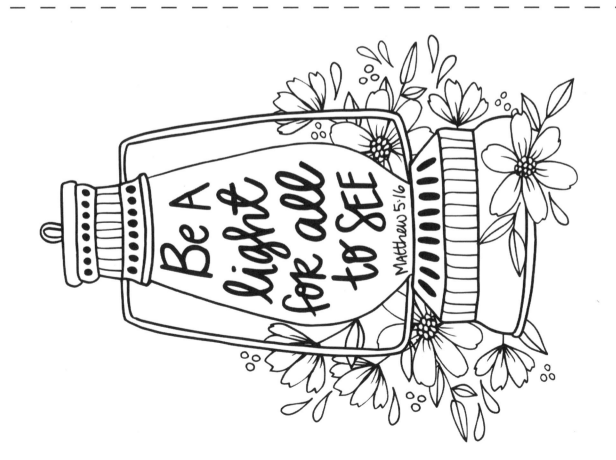

Be A light for all to SEE

Matthew 5:16

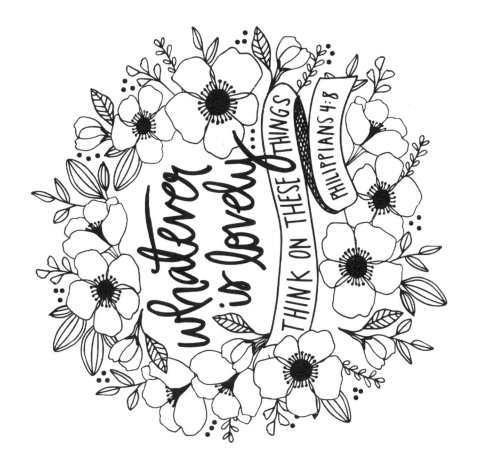

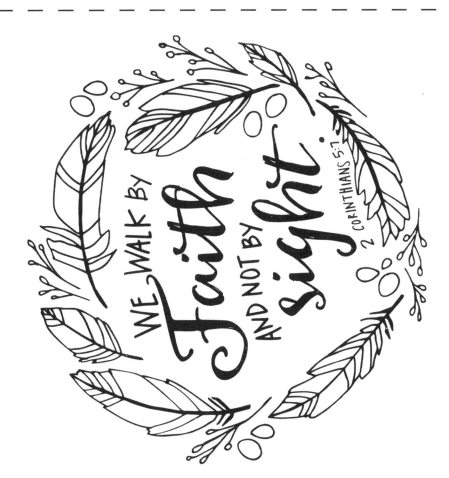

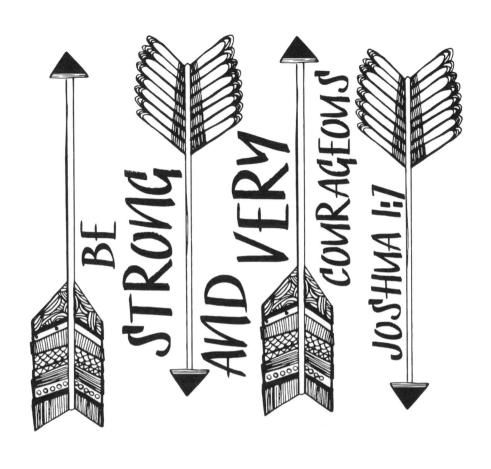

BE STRONG AND VERY COURAGEOUS

JOSHUA 1:7

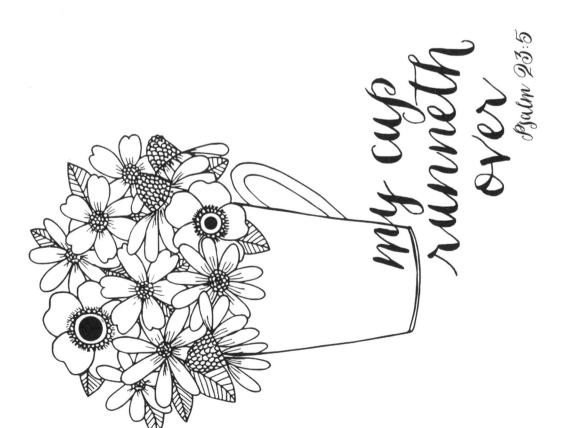

my cup runneth over

Psalm 23:5

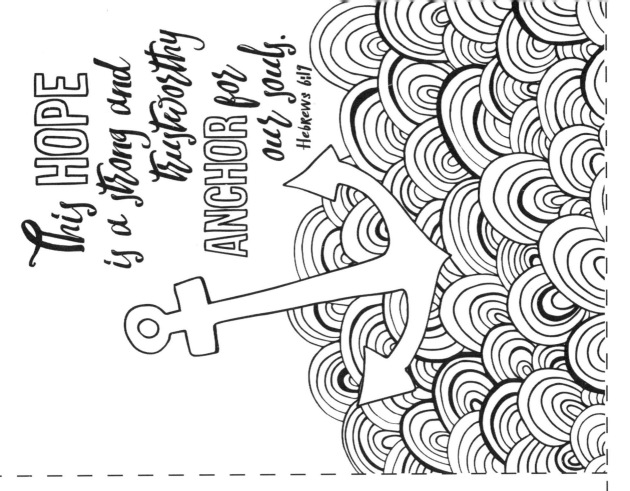

This HOPE is a strong and trustworthy ANCHOR for our souls. Hebrews 6:19

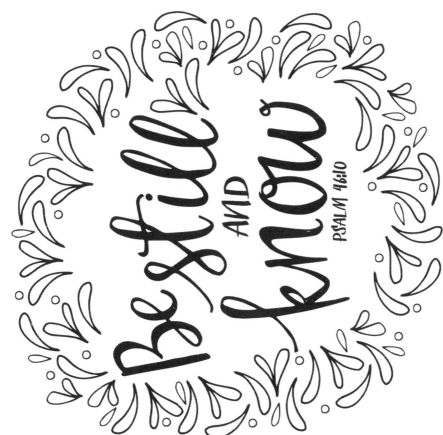

Be still AND know PSALM 46:10

PEN + PAINT

[Lindsay Hopkins]

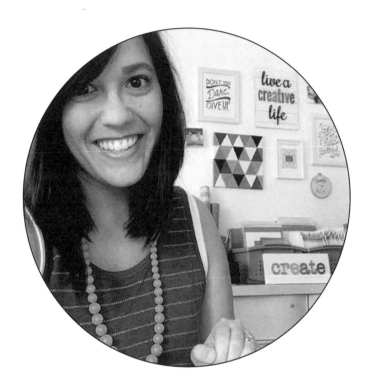

Artist and illustrator Lindsay Hopkins has been drawing and creating since childhood. She has a love for color and hopes to encourage and inspire others through her creativity.

Lindsay began her creative career in 2009 with custom painted canvases and nursery art. As she grew artistically Lindsay discovered new mediums and began illustrating. Her online shop, Pen & Paint, opened in 2012. Lindsay works out of her bright home studio in South Georgia creating inspirational art prints and stationery, along with other items featuring her artwork. [pen-and-paint.com]

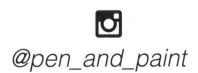

@pen_and_paint

paige tate
& CO.

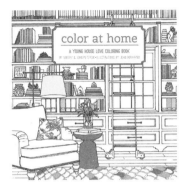

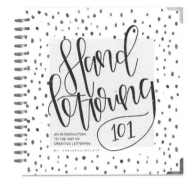

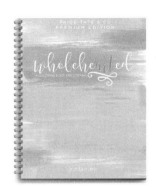

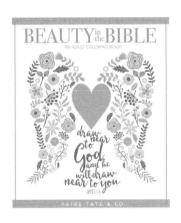

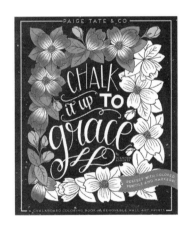

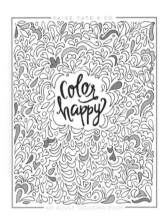

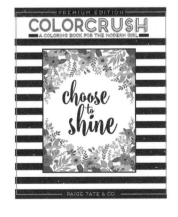

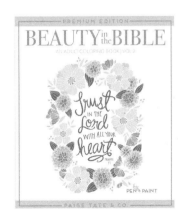

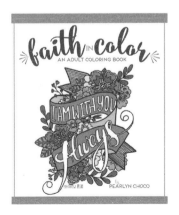